From the Institute of Medicine/
National Research Council Report

Confronting Commercial Sexual Exploitation
and
Sex Trafficking of Minors
in the United States

A Guide for Providers of Victim and Support Services

INSTITUTE OF MEDICINE *AND*
NATIONAL RESEARCH COUNCIL
OF THE NATIONAL ACADEMIES

D1559013

In 2013, the Institute of Medicine (IOM) and the National Research Council (NRC) published a report about commercial sexual exploitation and sex trafficking of minors in the United States. The report, *Confronting Commercial Sexual Exploitation and Sex Trafficking of Minors in the United States*, was funded by the U.S. Department of Justice Office of Juvenile Justice and Delinquency Prevention. It provides a comprehensive view of this issue and offers a detailed explanation of its findings and recommendations.

The content of this guide was derived entirely from the original report as an abridged version for providers of victim and support services. This guide, which was also funded by the U.S. Department of Justice Office of Juvenile Justice and Delinquency Prevention, was edited by Rona Briere and Patti Simon.

Confronting Commercial Sexual Exploitation and Sex Trafficking of Minors in the United States was authored by the IOM/NRC Committee on the Commercial Sexual Exploitation and Sex Trafficking of Minors in the United States:

ELLEN WRIGHT CLAYTON (*Co-Chair*), Craig-Weaver Professor of Pediatrics, Professor of Law, and Co-Founder, Center for Biomedical Ethics and Society, Vanderbilt University
RICHARD D. KRUGMAN (*Co-Chair*), Vice Chancellor for Health Affairs, University of Colorado School of Medicine
TONYA CHAFFEE, Medical Director of Child and Adolescent Support, Advocacy and Resource Center, University of California, San Francisco
ANGELA DIAZ, Jean C. and James W. Crystal Professor of Pediatrics and Preventive Medicine, Mount Sinai School of Medicine
ABIGAIL ENGLISH, Director, Center for Adolescent Health & the Law
BARBARA GUTHRIE, Associate Dean for Academic Affairs and Professor, Yale University School of Nursing
SHARON LAMBERT, Associate Professor of Clinical/Community Psychology, The George Washington University
MARK LATONERO, Research Director, Annenberg Center on Communication Leadership & Policy, University of Southern California
NATALIE McCLAIN, Assistant Professor, Boston College William F. Connell School of Nursing
CALLIE MARIE RENNISON, Associate Professor, School of Public Affairs, University of Colorado Denver
JOHN A. RICH, Professor and Chair of Health Management and Policy, Drexel University School of Public Health
JONATHAN TODRES, Professor of Law, Georgia State University College of Law
PATTI TOTH, Program Manager, Washington State Criminal Justice Training Commission

International Standard Book Number-13: 978-0-309-30489-4
International Standard Book Number-10: 0-309-30489-X

Additional copies of this report are available from the National Academies Press, 500 Fifth Street, NW, Keck 360, Washington, DC 20001; (800) 624-6242 or (202) 334-3313; http://www.nap.edu.

Contents

1 Introduction

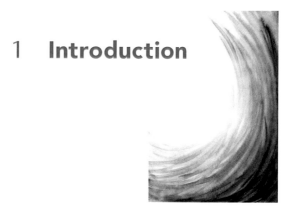

"Commercial sexual exploitation and sex trafficking of minors not only are illegal activities, but also result in immediate and long-term physical, mental, and emotional harm to victims and survivors."

Commercial sexual exploitation and sex trafficking of minors in the United States are frequently overlooked, misunderstood, and unaddressed domestic problems. In the past decade, they have received increasing attention from advocates, the media, academics, and policy makers. However, much of this attention has focused internationally. This international focus has overshadowed the reality that commercial sexual exploitation and sex trafficking of minors also occur every day within the United States.

Commercial sexual exploitation and sex trafficking of minors not only are illegal activities, but also result in immediate and long-term physical, mental, and emotional harm to victims and survivors. A nation that is unaware of these problems or disengaged from solving them unwittingly contributes to the ongoing abuse of minors and all but ensures that these crimes will remain marginalized and misunderstood.

PURPOSE OF THIS GUIDE

In September 2013, the Institute of Medicine (IOM) and the National Research Council (NRC) of the National Academies published the report *Confronting*

Commercial Sexual Exploitation and Sex Trafficking of Minors in the United States.
The purpose of that report is to:

- increase awareness and understanding of the crucial problem of
  commercial sexual exploitation and sex trafficking of minors in the
  United States;
- examine emerging strategies for preventing and identifying these
  crimes, for assisting and supporting victims and survivors, and for
  addressing exploiters and traffickers; and
- offer a path forward through recommendations designed to increase
  awareness and understanding and to support efforts to prevent,
  identify, and respond to these crimes.

The IOM/NRC report includes chapters on specific sectors with a role to
play in addressing the problem. Because the report is lengthy and broad in
its reach, the IOM/NRC, with the support of the U.S. Department of Justice
Office of Juvenile Justice and Delinquency Prevention, decided to develop
a series of guides offering a more concise and focused perspective on the
problem and emerging solutions for several of these sectors.

INTENDED AUDIENCE

The intended audience for this guide is providers[1] of victim and support
services for children and adolescents who have experienced or are at risk of
commercial sexual exploitation and sex trafficking. These service providers
include individuals (policy makers, leaders, practitioners), organizations, and
programs at the local, state, and federal levels. They encompass child welfare
and child protective services, other agencies and programs within the state
and federal governments (e.g., the U.S. Department of Justice's Office for
Victims of Crime), and nongovernmental organizations.

HOW THIS GUIDE IS ORGANIZED

Following this introduction, Section 2 provides definitions of relevant terms,
a set of guiding principles, a summary of what is known about the extent of
the problem, and an overview of risk factors and consequences.
    Section 3 describes some emerging strategies for preventing and re-
sponding to these crimes. It describes both strategies specific to the victim

---

[1] Note that throughout this guide, the term "provider" is intended to encompass all of the
entities—from individuals to organizations—that make up the victim and support services
sector.

and support services sector and multisector, collaborative strategies in which providers of victim and support services play a role.

Section 4 reviews approaches to providing services for victims and survivors of these crimes, including trauma-informed care, case management, and survivor-led and survivor-informed models. It also describes several key challenges to service provision.

Finally, Section 5 presents strategies for making progress in identifying, preventing, and responding to these crimes, based on the recommendations offered in the IOM/NRC report.

2 The Problem

"Commercial sexual exploitation and sex trafficking
of minors should be understood as acts of abuse and
violence against children and adolescents."

This chapter first defines terms relevant to the problem of commercial sexual exploitation and sex trafficking of minors in the United States. It then presents a set of guiding principles that should inform any efforts to address the problem. Next is a brief discussion of what is known about the extent of the problem. The final section summarizes the current understanding of risk factors and consequences. One of the messages that emerges from this discussion is that, while the gravity of the problem is clear, critical gaps in the knowledge base for understanding and addressing it need to be filled.

THE DEFINITION ISSUE

The language used to describe aspects of commercial sexual exploitation and sex trafficking crimes and their victims and survivors—a collection of terms derived from the range of agencies, sectors, and individuals working to prevent and address these crimes—varies considerably. Some terms are diagnostic and scientific (e.g., *screening* and *medical forensic exam*). Others are legal terms (e.g., *trafficking*, *offender*, *perpetrator*). Some terms are used frequently in popular culture (e.g., *pimp*, *john*, *child prostitute*). Still others are focused on the experiences of exploited children (e.g., *victim, survivor, modern-day slavery*). The result is the absence of a shared language regarding commercial sexual exploitation and sex trafficking of minors.

The implications of this absence of a common language can be significant. For example, a child or adolescent victim identified as a prostitute may be treated as a criminal and detained, whereas the same youth identified as a victim of commercial sexual exploitation will be referred for a range of health and protective services. Box 1 provides the definition used in the IOM/NRC report for the commercial sexual exploitation and sex trafficking of minors. Box 2 presents the report's definitions for some of the more common terms related to these crimes.

Commercial sexual exploitation and *sex trafficking* of minors are distinct but overlapping terms. Indeed, disentangling commercial sexual exploitation from sex trafficking is impossible in many instances. Two points are particularly important for readers of this guide. First, programs designed for victims and survivors will need to account for a range of experiences and needs among those being served. Second, as reflected in the guiding principles presented in the next section, it is crucial to recognize and understand commercial sexual exploitation and sex trafficking of minors as part of a broader pattern of child abuse (as illustrated by Figure 1).

BOX 1
Definition of Commercial Sexual Exploitation
and Sex Trafficking of Minors

Commercial sexual exploitation and *sex trafficking of minors* encompass a range of crimes of a sexual nature committed against children and adolescents, including

- recruiting, enticing, harboring, transporting, providing, obtaining, and/or maintaining (acts that constitute trafficking) a minor for the purpose of sexual exploitation;
- exploiting a minor through prostitution;
- exploiting a minor through survival sex (exchanging sex/sexual acts for money or something of value, such as shelter, food, or drugs);
- using a minor in pornography;
- exploiting a minor through sex tourism, mail order bride trade, and early marriage; and
- exploiting a minor by having her/him perform in sexual venues (e.g., peep shows or strip clubs).

BOX 2
Definitions of Other Key Terms

Minors—Refers to individuals under age 18.

Prostituted child—Used instead of *child prostitute, juvenile prostitute,* and *adolescent prostitute,* which suggest that prostituted children are willing participants in an illegal activity. As stated in the guiding principles in the text below, these young people should be recognized as victims, not criminals.

Traffickers, exploiters, and pimps—used to describe individuals who exploit children sexually for financial or other gain. In today's slang, pimp is often used to describe something as positive or glamorous. Therefore, the IOM/NRC report instead uses the terms trafficker and exploiter to describe individuals who sell children and adolescents for sex. It is also important to note that traffickers and exploiters come in many forms; they may be family members, intimate partners, or friends, as well as strangers.

Victims and survivors—Refers to minors who are commercially sexually exploited or trafficked for sexual purposes. The terms are not mutually exclusive, but can be applied to the same individual at different points along a continuum. The term *victim* indicates that a crime has occurred and that assistance is needed. Being able to identify an individual as a victim, even temporarily, can help activate responses—including direct services and legal protections—for an individual. The term *survivor* is also used because it can have therapeutic value, and the label *victim* may be counterproductive at times.

GUIDING PRINCIPLES

"Minors who are commercially sexually exploited or trafficked for sexual purposes should not be considered criminals."

The IOM/NRC report offers the following guiding principles as an essential foundation for understanding and responding to commercial sexual exploitation and sex trafficking of minors:

- Commercial sexual exploitation and sex trafficking of minors should be understood as acts of abuse and violence against children and adolescents.
- Minors who are commercially sexually exploited or trafficked for sexual purposes should not be considered criminals.
- Identification of victims and survivors and any intervention, above all, should do no further harm to any child or adolescent.

FIGURE 1 Commercial sexual exploitation and sex trafficking of minors are forms of child abuse.
NOTE: This diagram is for illustrative purposes only; it does not indicate or imply percentages.

EXTENT OF THE PROBLEM

> "Despite the current imperfect estimates, commercial sexual exploitation and sex trafficking of minors in the United States clearly are problems of grave concern."

Despite the gravity of commercial sexual exploitation and sex trafficking of minors in the United States, these crimes currently are not well understood or adequately addressed. Many factors contribute to this lack of understanding. For example:

- Commercial sexual exploitation and sex trafficking of minors in the United States may be overlooked and underreported because they frequently occur at the margins of society and behind closed doors. Their victims are often vulnerable to exploitation. They include children who are, or have been, neglected or abused; those in foster care or juvenile detention; and those who are homeless, runaways (i.e., children who leave home without permission), or so-called thrownaways (i.e., children and adolescents who are asked or told to leave home). Thus, children and adolescents affected by commercial sexual exploitation and sex trafficking can be difficult to reach.

- The absence of specific policies and protocols related to commercial sexual exploitation and sex trafficking of minors, coupled with a lack of specialized training, makes it difficult to identify—and thus count—victims and survivors of these crimes.
- Victims and survivors may be distrustful of law enforcement, may not view themselves as "victims," or may be too traumatized to report or disclose the crimes committed against them.
- Most states continue to arrest commercially exploited children and adolescents as criminals instead of treating them as victims, and health care providers and educators have not widely adopted screening for commercial sexual exploitation and sex trafficking of minors. A lack of awareness among those who routinely interact with victims and survivors ensures that these crimes are not identified and properly addressed.

As a result of these factors, the true scope of commercial sexual exploitation and sex trafficking of minors within the United States is difficult to quantify, and estimates of the incidence and prevalence of commercial sexual exploitation and sex trafficking of minors in the United States are scarce. Further, there is little to no consensus on the value of existing estimates. This lack of consensus is not unusual and indeed is the case for estimates of other crimes as well (e.g., rape and intimate partner violence).

The IOM/NRC report maintains that, despite the current imperfect estimates, commercial sexual exploitation and sex trafficking of minors in the United States clearly are problems of grave concern. Therefore, the report's recommendations go beyond refining national estimates of commercial sexual exploitation and sex trafficking of minors in the United States to emphasize that unless additional resources become available existing resources should be focused on what can be done to assist the victims of these crimes.

RISK FACTORS

Risk factors for victims of commercial sexual exploitation and sex trafficking of minors have been identified at the individual, family, peer, neighborhood, and societal levels (see Figure 2).[1] Adding to this complexity, these risk factors, as well as corresponding protective factors, interact within and across levels.

---

[1]It should be noted that the evidence base for risk factors, as well as for consequences (discussed in this section) is very limited. Therefore, the IOM/NRC report draws heavily on related literature (such as child maltreatment, sexual assault/rape, and trauma), as well as evidence gathered through workshops and site visits.

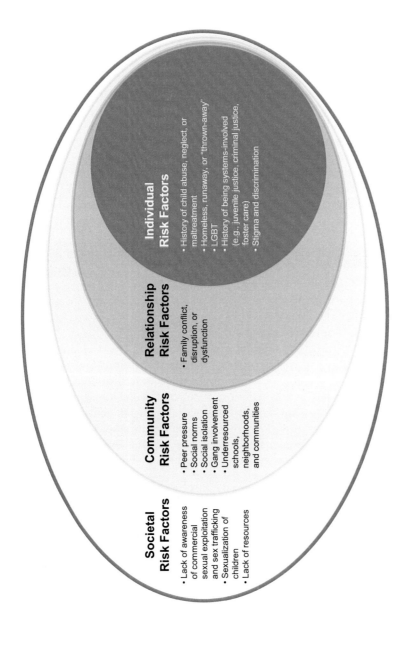

FIGURE 2 Possible risk factors for commercial sexual exploitation and sex trafficking of minors.
NOTE: LGBT = lesbian, gay, bisexual, or transgender.

Figure 2 highlights the complex and interconnected forces that contribute to commercial sexual exploitation and sex trafficking of minors. It should be noted, however, that the factors shown are likely only a subset of the risk factors for these crimes. Moreover, these factors do not operate alone. For example, the presence of one or more risk factors would not result in the commercial sexual exploitation and sex trafficking of minors without the presence of an exploiter or trafficker. The factors depicted in Figure 2 may function independently of one another or in combination. In addition, risk factors in one sphere may trigger a cascade of effects or initiate pathways into or out of commercial sexual exploitation and sex trafficking.

Finally, the factors in Figure 2 may also be risks for other types of adverse youth outcomes. Therefore, their presence does not necessarily signal commercial sexual exploitation and sex trafficking of minors, but should be considered as part of a more comprehensive assessment to determine youth at risk of or involved in these crimes.

Box 3 summarizes findings from the IOM/NRC report that highlight the risk factors depicted in Figure 2.

CONSEQUENCES

> "Overall, research suggests that victims and survivors of commercial sexual exploitation and sex trafficking face developmental, social, societal, and legal consequences that have both short- and long-term impacts on their health and well-being."

The available literature shows that child maltreatment, particularly child sexual abuse, has significant negative impacts on the physical health, mental health, and social functioning of victims in adulthood, and leads to increased health risk behaviors and mental health problems among adolescents. While studies focused on consequences for commercially sexually exploited children and adolescents are rare, the data based on child sexual abuse are useful given evidence that these problems are linked in some cases. Overall, research suggests that victims and survivors of commercial sexual exploitation and sex trafficking face developmental, social, societal, and legal consequences that have both short- and long-term impacts on their health and well-being.

BOX 3
Findings on Risk Factors

- Child maltreatment, particularly sexual abuse, is strongly associated with commercial sexual exploitation and sex trafficking of minors.
- Psychogenic factors, such as poor self-esteem, chronic depression, and external locus of control, in addition to low future orientation, may be risk factors for involvement in these crimes. This possible link is supported by the association between child maltreatment and these psychogenic factors.
- Off-schedule developmental phenomena, such as early pubertal maturation, early sexual participation, and early work initiation, have negative consequences for youth.
- While commercial sexual exploitation and sex trafficking can affect youth across the board, some groups are at higher risk, including those who lack stable housing (because of being homeless, runaways, or "thrown aways") and sexual and gender minority youth. In addition, some settings and situations—homelessness, foster care placement, and juvenile justice involvement—are particularly high risk under certain circumstances, providing opportunities for recruitment.
- Substance use/abuse is a risk factor for commercial sexual exploitation and sex trafficking of minors and also may perpetuate exploitation.
- The sexualization of children, particularly girls, in U.S. society and the perception that involvement in sex after puberty is consensual, contribute to the commercial sexual exploitation and sex trafficking of minors.
- Disability should be considered a vulnerability for involvement in these crimes given its association with child sexual abuse.
- Online and digital technologies are part of a complex social system that includes both risk factors (recruiting, grooming, and advertising victims) and protective factors (identifying, monitoring, and combating exploiters) for these crimes.
- Beyond child maltreatment, the experience of childhood adversity, such as growing up in a home with a family member with mental illness or substance abuse or having an incarcerated parent, may increase the risk for involvement in commercial sexual exploitation and sex trafficking of minors.
- Peer pressure and modeling can influence a youth's entry into (or avoidance of) commercial sexual exploitation.
- The neighborhood context—such as community norms about sexual behavior and what constitutes consent and coercion, and whether the community is characterized by poverty, crime, police corruption, adult prostitution, and high numbers of transient males—can increase the risk for involvement in these crimes.

3 How Victim and Support Services Can Help

By definition, all victim and support service professionals work with vulnerable and victimized youth. Minors who have experienced or are at risk of commercial sexual exploitation and sex trafficking are often subject to other forms of abuse and may be receiving victim and support services in connection with that abuse. Therefore, victim and support service professionals should be able to recognize past, ongoing, or potential victimization by commercial sexual exploitation and sex trafficking among the youth in their care. Failure to recognize victims and survivors of these crimes is not uncommon among these professionals, however [1, 2]. As a result, those at risk may become victims, and victims may miss opportunities for assistance and remain vulnerable to further exploitation and abuse.

This section describes some noteworthy examples of efforts by child welfare and governmental and nongovernmental victim and support service organizations that show promise as ways of preventing these crimes and providing victims and survivors with the help they need. At the same time, however, the IOM/NRC report emphasizes that no one sector, discipline, or area of practice can fully understand or respond effectively to the complex problems surrounding these crimes; collaboration and coordination among multiple sectors and agencies are necessary to mount an adequate response. Therefore, this section also describes examples of multisector and interagency collaborations in which victim and support services play a role.

Before proceeding, it must be emphasized that none of the efforts described here have undergone sufficient research and evaluation to be recommended for replication. The need for further research and evaluation of all strategies for addressing commercial sexual exploitation and sex trafficking of minors is a key theme in Section 5 on recommended strategies for progress.

> "No one sector, discipline, or area of practice can fully understand or respond effectively to the complex problems surrounding these crimes; collaboration and coordination among multiple sectors and agencies are necessary to mount an adequate response."

CHILD WELFARE

As noted in Section 2, involvement in the child welfare system, including out-of-home placement, such as in group homes and foster care, may be a risk factor for commercial sexual exploitation and sex trafficking of minors. Understanding the potential risks related to involvement in the child welfare system can help child welfare professionals recognize and address those risks and potentially prevent these crimes among youth already involved in the system.

While one of the primary responsibilities of child welfare is to prevent the abuse, neglect, and exploitation of children, this responsibility traditionally has not been applied to extrafamilial victimization, which generally has fallen within the purview of law enforcement [3, p. 2]. As emphasized in Section 1, commercial sexual exploitation and sex trafficking of minors, at their core, are forms of child abuse. Child welfare agencies, therefore, have a responsibility to assist victims and survivors of these crimes. In addition, child welfare caseworkers may serve an important role as "gateway providers" to supportive services for victims and survivors of abuse [4].

The IOM/NRC report offers specific examples of efforts to enhance the involvement of child welfare in addressing these crimes. They include creating a specific "allegation of harm" for commercial sexual exploitation and sex trafficking of minors to improve case management, requiring reporting to child protective services, raising awareness and building capacity in child welfare, and developing state guidelines and tools for child welfare professionals.

> "Commercial sexual exploitation and sex trafficking of minors, at their core, are forms of child abuse. Child welfare agencies, therefore, have a responsibility to assist victims and survivors of these crimes."

BOX 4
Creating an Allegation of Harm for Commercial
Sexual Exploitation and Sex Trafficking of Minors

The Illinois Safe Children Act includes "human trafficking of children" as an allegation of harm in the Statewide Automated Child Welfare Information System, a central data collection point that helps maintain a complete case management history of child maltreatment. The law stipulates that victims of commercial sexual exploitation and sex trafficking of minors should be considered "abused," so that when an individual under age 18 is taken into custody for a prostitution offense, law enforcement must notify the Illinois Department of Children and Family Services of the allegation of human trafficking. The Department of Children and Family Services, in turn, is required to open an investigation into the abuse within 24 hours of the initial report.

FOR MORE INFORMATION:

Children's Bureau. 2012. About SACWIS/TACWIS.
http://www.acf.hhs.gov/programs/cb/research-data-technology/state-tribal-info-systems/ about

State of Illinois Department of Children and Family Services. 2011. Allegation of Harm #40/90 Human Trafficking of Children.
http://www.state.il.us/dcfs/docs/ocfp/policy/Policy_Guide_2013.05.pdf

Creating an "Allegation of Harm"

Several states, including Connecticut, Florida, and Illinois, have designated human trafficking as a specific abuse allegation, as distinct from other reported types of child maltreatment (e.g., domestic violence, sexual abuse, incest, or other forms of physical abuse) (see Box 4). This designation can help officials collect and analyze state-level data and coordinate case management for victims.

Requiring Reporting to Child Protective Services

In Massachusetts, all suspected cases of commercial sexual exploitation and sex trafficking of minors must be referred to child protective services [5]. A report to child protective services prompts referral to a case coordinator, which, in turn, activates a comprehensive, coordinated response to the victim/survivor.

FOR MORE INFORMATION:

Suffolk County Massachusetts' Response to Commercial Sexual Exploitation of Children (CSEC). 2012.
http://www.suffolkcac.org/assets/pdf/From_the_Life_to_My_Life_Suffolk_Countys_Response_to_CSEC_June_2012.pdf

Raising Awareness and Building Capacity in Child Welfare

As noted earlier, the role of child welfare in addressing the commercial sexual exploitation and sex trafficking of minors may be limited by the failure to recognize victims and survivors of these crimes and by the perception that victims should be handled in the juvenile justice system [2, 6]. The International Organization for Adolescents and the Center for the Human Rights of Children at Loyola University Chicago, in partnership with the Illinois Department of Children and Family Services, developed the *Building Child Welfare Response to Child Trafficking Handbook* [2]. The purpose of this handbook is to help child welfare agencies fulfill their responsibility of identifying and serving trafficking victims as required by the Illinois Safe Children Act.

FOR MORE INFORMATION:

The International Organization for Adolescents and the Center for the Human Rights of Children at Loyola University Chicago. 2011. Building Child Welfare Response to Child Trafficking Handbook.
http://www.luc.edu/media/lucedu/chrc/pdfs/BCWRHandbook2011.pdf

Developing State Guidelines and Tools for Child Welfare Professionals

The State of Florida's Department of Children and Family Services has developed specific guidelines to assist child welfare and child protection professionals with reporting allegations of human trafficking of children. In addition, the state developed a tool to assist child protection investigators in identifying trafficking victims. Currently, guidance of this nature is lacking at the federal level and within most states.

FOR MORE INFORMATION:

State of Florida Department of Children and Families. 2009. Human Trafficking of Children Indicator Tool.
http://www.dcf.state.fl.us/programs/humantrafficking//docs/Human TraffickingOfChildrenIndicatoTool0109.pdf

State of Florida Department of Children and Families. 2009. Intakes and Investigative Response to Human Trafficking of Children.
http://centerforchildwelfare2.fmhi.usf.edu/kb/DCF_Pol/Family%20
Safety%20CFOP's/175-14HumanTrafficking2013.pdf

FEDERAL AND STATE GOVERNMENTS

The federal government addresses the commercial sexual exploitation and sex trafficking of minors by providing support for services, training, technical assistance, outreach to increase public awareness, and information resources. Examples include making federal benefits and services available to trafficking victims, funding service organizations, and providing employment and job training to trafficking victims. At the state level, governments can help address the problem by using a statewide coordinated care approach to the provision of victim and support services.

Making Federal Benefits and Services Available to Victims of Trafficking

Efforts of the U.S. Department of Health and Human Services (HHS) include regional training and meetings; outreach efforts to raise public awareness (e.g., the Rescue & Restore Victims of Human Trafficking campaign); technical assistance to program grantees who work with victims of human trafficking; and funding for the National Human Trafficking Resource Center, a national resource for victims of human trafficking and the public. In addition, HHS developed a guide to federal benefits and services available to trafficking victims [7]. This resource provides program-by-program information on benefits and services and includes eligibility requirements.

The President's Interagency Task Force to Monitor and Combat Trafficking in Persons recently released a 5-year federal strategic action plan on services for victims of human trafficking in the United States. Among its goals, the plan calls for expanding access to services from a range of agencies for victims of human trafficking throughout the United States.

FOR MORE INFORMATION:

Rescue and Restore Victims of Human Trafficking Campaign.
http://www.acf.hhs.gov/programs/orr/resource/about-rescue-restore

National Human Trafficking Resource Center.
http://www.acf.hhs.gov/programs/orr/resource/fact-sheet-national-human-trafficking-resource-center

Services Available to Victims of Human Trafficking.
http://www.acf.hhs.gov/sites/default/files/orr/traffickingservices_0.pdf

U.S. Department of State. 2012. Annual Meeting of the President's Interagency Task Force to Monitor and Combat Trafficking in Persons.
http://www.state.gov/j/tip/rls/reports/pitf/

President's Interagency Task Force to Monitor and Combat Trafficking in Persons. 2013. Federal Strategic Action Plan on Services for Victims of Human Trafficking in the United States 2013-2017.
http://ideascale.com//userimages/accounts/91/912839/Victim-Services-SAP-2013-04-09-Public-Comment-B.pdf

Funding Service Organizations

The U.S. Department of Justice provides funding to victim services organizations at the local, regional, and national levels through grants made by the Office for Victims of Crime. The 2013 reauthorization of the Trafficking Victims Protection Act (TVPA) has supplemented these programs by authorizing HHS to issue up to four grants to state or local entities, with the requirement that two-thirds of the funding be used for residential care and services for victims and survivors of sex trafficking who are minors. Funds are also used to develop interagency partnerships and public outreach and awareness campaigns.

FOR MORE INFORMATION:

Grants Made by Office for Victims of Crime.
http://ojp.gov/ovc/grants

Reauthorization of Trafficking Victims Protection Act.
http://www.state.gov/j/tip/laws

U.S. Department of State. 2012. Annual Meeting of the President's Interagency Task Force to Monitor and Combat Trafficking in Persons.
http://www.state.gov/j/tip/rls/reports/pitf/

Providing Employment and Job Training to Trafficking Victims

The U.S. Department of Labor offers employment and training services to trafficking victims, as required by the TVPA. In addition, the TVPA stipulates that victims of convicted traffickers are entitled to full restitution for the labor they performed.

FOR MORE INFORMATION:

U.S. Department of State. 2012. Annual Meeting of the President's Interagency Task Force to Monitor and Combat Trafficking in Persons. http://www.state.gov/j/tip/rls/reports/pitf/

Using a Statewide Coordinated Care Approach to the Provision of Victim and Support Services

Georgia Care Connection was established by Georgia's Governor's Office for Children and Families to serve as a central, statewide hub for victims and survivors of commercial sexual exploitation and sex trafficking of minors and for professionals (e.g., law enforcement personnel, school personnel, child welfare professionals, health care providers) seeking to help them. Through a broad network of state and local service providers and professionals, Georgia Care Connection coordinates a "comprehensive care plan" for victims and survivors. This comprehensive plan integrates and coordinates prevention, intervention, and treatment services (e.g., legal, mental and physical health, housing) that are guided by the specific needs of each victim/survivor.

FOR MORE INFORMATION:

Georgia Care Connection. http://children.georgia.gov/task-force-overview

Nongovernmental Organizations

Nongovernmental organizations (NGOs) serving victims and survivors of commercial sexual exploitation and sex trafficking of minors include specialized direct service providers, faith-based organizations, service providers and community organizations that serve other populations, advocacy organizations, and private foundations, among others. These organizations help address the problem through curriculum development and education, training for victim and support service professionals, direct care and services, outreach and public awareness initiatives, prevention efforts, hotlines, and direct support to state and local organizations.

Curriculum Development and Education

A number of NGOs have developed and implemented curricula designed to reach current and potential victims and survivors of commercial sexual exploitation and sex trafficking of minors. One example is described in Box 5.

Training for Victim and Support Service Professionals

Some NGOs have developed and implemented training for victim and support service professionals who work with minors that have experienced or are at risk of commercial sexual exploitation and sex trafficking. One example, Girls Educational & Mentoring Services (GEMS), is described in Box 6. Other examples of organizations that conduct training for an array of victim and support service providers include Motivating, Inspiring, Supporting, and Serving Sexually Exploited Youth; Polaris Project; Standing Against Global Exploitation; and Shared Hope International.

BOX 5
My Life, My Choice

My Life, My Choice (MLMC) is an educational curriculum developed by the Boston-based My Life, My Choice initiative, which works to identify and intervene with adolescent girls who are vulnerable to commercial sexual exploitation and sex trafficking [8]. The MLMC curriculum consists of 10 sessions led and facilitated by trained staff, typically a licensed clinician and a survivor of commercial sexual exploitation or sex trafficking. The curriculum can be delivered in a variety of settings (e.g., group homes and residential facilities, child protective services offices, juvenile justice facilities, community-based organizations).

The goals of the curriculum include preventing commercial sexual exploitation and sex trafficking among at-risk adolescents and preventing revictimization among those previously exploited. The curriculum was designed to alter participants' behavior by changing their attitudes, knowledge, and skills (i.e., improving attitudes regarding sexual health and self-esteem, increasing knowledge of the relationship between substance use and commercial sexual exploitation and sex trafficking, and developing skills to access resources and recognize potential exploiters) [9].

FOR MORE INFORMATION:

My Life, My Choice (MLMC).
http://jri.org/services/behavioral-health-and-trauma-services/community-based-behavioral-health-services/my-life-my-choice

BOX 6
Girls Educational & Mentoring Services (GEMS)

GEMS, a New York City–based nonprofit organization that provides services to girls and young women (aged 12 to 24) who have experienced commercial sexual exploitation and sex trafficking, has developed and implemented two curricula for organizations working with victims and survivors of these crimes.

The first, the Office of Juvenile Justice and Delinquency Prevention's Commercial Sexual Exploitation of Children Community Intervention Project Train-the-Trainer curriculum, is designed to provide an overview of issues related to commercial sexual exploitation and sex trafficking of minors for victim and support service providers, law enforcement personnel, health care professionals, child welfare professionals, legal professionals (e.g., prosecutors, legal aid professionals/public defenders, family court officials), school personnel, and first responders. Specific topics include prevention and identification strategies, assessment and counseling techniques, and investigation and interviewing strategies, among others.

Second, the Victim, Survivor, Leader™ curriculum is designed to assist organizations interested in developing and providing "specialized services" for female victims and survivors of commercial sexual exploitation and sex trafficking.

In addition to these two curricula, GEMS offers technical assistance to organizations seeking additional guidance on the design and delivery of services to the victims and survivors of commercial sexual exploitation and sex trafficking.

FOR MORE INFORMATION:

GEMS (Girls Educational & Mentoring Services). 2013. Training and Technical Assistance. http://www.gems-girls.org/get-trained/training-and-technical-assistance

Direct Care and Services

Various organizations provide direct care and services to victims and survivors of commercial sexual exploitation and sex trafficking of minors. These services include temporary and longer-term shelter, intensive case management, victim outreach, support groups, counseling and therapeutic services, mentoring, and legal assistance. Two examples are described in Box 7.

Several direct care service providers also focus on specific vulnerable populations, such as boys/adolescent males; lesbian, gay, bisexual, or transgender (LGBT) youth; and homeless youth. As discussed in Section 4, boys/adolescent males and LGBT youth are often overlooked as populations at risk for commercial sexual exploitation and sex trafficking. As a result, victim and support services for these youth are especially scarce. One example of an effort to meet this need is Larkin Street Youth Services, a San Francisco–based

**BOX 7
Examples of Direct Care and Services
for Victims and Survivors**

Courtney's House is a survivor-run organization that provides services to victims and survivors of commercial sexual exploitation and sex trafficking of minors in the Washington, DC, metropolitan area [10]. Services include case management; educational assistance; survivor-led support groups for male, female, and transgender victims and survivors; mentorship programs; counseling; group therapy; and academic tutoring. In addition, an overnight street outreach program is aimed at identifying victims, survivors, and minors who are at risk of commercial sexual exploitation or sex trafficking. Finally, Courtney's House maintains a hotline staffed by victims and survivors of these crimes.

FOR MORE INFORMATION:

Courtney's House.
http://www.courtneyshouse.org

The Salvation Army's STOP-IT Initiative Against Human Trafficking provides services to victims of human trafficking in 11 counties in Illinois [11]. The program creates individualized service plans for victims and survivors and provides referrals for shelter and housing, transportation, legal services, medical care, mental health services, education, and employment services.

FOR MORE INFORMATION:

The Salvation Army's STOP-IT Initiative Against Human Trafficking.
http://sa-stopit.org

nonprofit organization that provides a range of support services to homeless and runaway youth aged 13 to 24, many of whom are male, LGBT, or questioning [12]. Larkin Street provides underage emergency shelter, transitional living programs, primary medical care, case management, education and employment services, HIV prevention information and testing, mental health services, and substance abuse intervention [1]. In addition, Larkin Street collaborates with other area service providers that serve primarily girls and women to make services available to those it may be unable to assist.

FOR MORE INFORMATION:

Larkin Street Youth Services.
http://www.larkinstreetyouth.org

Other examples of organizations that serve boys and LGBT and questioning youth include the Center on Halsted, Courtney's House (discussed in Box 7), and Boston Gay & Lesbian Adolescent Social Services.

FOR MORE INFORMATION:

Center on Halsted.
https://www.centeronhalsted.org

Boston GLASS (Boston Gay & Lesbian Adolescent Social Services). 2013. Services.
http://www.jri.org/services/health-hiv-lgbtq-services/health-and-prevention-services/boston-glass/services

> "Boys/adolescent males and LGBT youth are often overlooked as populations at risk for commercial sexual exploitation and sex trafficking. As a result, victim and support services for these youth are especially scarce."

Outreach and Public Awareness Initiatives

A number of NGOs have created outreach campaigns to raise public awareness of commercial sexual exploitation and sex trafficking of minors in the United States. Three national-level examples are Shared Hope International, Polaris Project, and ECPAT-USA:

- **Shared Hope International** has worked to increase public awareness of these crimes by producing a series of reports focused on demand [13], domestic sex trafficking of minors [14], and state-by-state legal responses [15]; by using various media (e.g., billboard campaigns and YouTube videos); and by holding national conferences and public events.

  FOR MORE INFORMATION:

  Shared Hope International.
  http://sharedhope.org

- **Polaris Project** operates the National Human Trafficking Resource Center. The Polaris Project website includes downloadable resources for the public, a range of service providers and professionals, victims and survivors, and individuals at risk for human trafficking. These resources include information on existing and pending federal- and state-level legislation on human trafficking, downloadable flyers that publicize the National Human Trafficking Resource Center's hotline number (translated in 20 languages), an online directory of selected state-by-state resources, and general information about commercial sexual exploitation and sex trafficking of minors.

FOR MORE INFORMATION:

National Human Trafficking Resource Center.
http://www.polarisproject.org/what-we-do/national-human-trafficking-hotline/the-nhtrc/overview

- In addition to providing resources on its website, **ECPAT-USA** organizes a youth-led educational outreach program, the Youth Committee, that engages high school students in efforts to address commercial sexual exploitation and sex trafficking of minors. In addition, ECPAT-USA's Tourism Child-Protection Code of Conduct provides a set of principles that encourage domestic travel and tourism companies to adopt policies addressing these crimes [16].

FOR MORE INFORMATION:

ECPAT-USA (End Child Prostitution and Trafficking-United States of America). 2013. Youth Committee: Involving Young People in Ending Trafficking.
http://www.ecpatusa.org/overview

ECPAT-USA. 2013. About the Code: The Tourism Child-Protection Code of Conduct.
http://www.ecpatusa.org/6012/code

In addition to these national-level examples, many other NGOs engage in outreach and public awareness campaigns using a range of strategies, including testimony before Congress, print and media campaigns, and presentations to community-based groups.

Prevention Efforts

Most current prevention efforts focus on raising awareness of the problem of commercial sexual exploitation and sex trafficking of minors and improving capacity to identify children and adolescents at risk of victimization (the curricula described in Box 6, developed by GEMS, are examples). Other organizations' prevention work is aimed primarily at assisting and supporting those at risk for commercial sexual exploitation and sex trafficking (GEMS and MLMC, described in Box 5, are examples). At least one organization has focused on educating adolescent males. The Chicago Alliance Against Sexual Exploitation (CAASE) created Empowering Young Men to End Sexual Exploitation, a prevention program for adolescent males that is implemented in Chicago-area high schools [17].

Additional prevention strategies are aimed at deterring and eliminating demand by promoting victim- and survivor-centered law enforcement strategies and laws. For example, End Demand Illinois, a statewide campaign of CAASE, supports the creation of new laws and resources for law enforcement to facilitate the arrest, filing of charges against, and prosecution of exploiters.

FOR MORE INFORMATION:

Empowering Young Men to End Sexual Exploitation.
http://caase.org/prevention

End Demand Illinois. 2013. Campaign Goals.
http://www.enddemandillinois.org/campaign-goals

Hotlines

Various hotlines (or help lines) are operated to assist victims of human trafficking; provide referrals; and, to the extent possible, connect individuals with support services in their communities. Examples are described in Box 8.

Direct Support to State and Local Organizations

Some statewide community foundations directly support the efforts of state and local organizations to prevent and respond to commercial sexual exploitation and sex trafficking of minors. One example is the Women's Foundation of Minnesota, which in 2011 launched the 5-year "Minnesota Girls Are Not for Sale" campaign to support services, research, and public education on commercial sexual exploitation and sex trafficking of girls. Grantees have included local governments and nonprofit organizations.

FOR MORE INFORMATION:

Women's Foundation of Minnesota. 2011. Women's Foundation of Minnesota Launches Campaign to End the Prostitution of Minnesota Girls.
http://www.wfmn.org/PDFs/WFM_MNGirls_Nov12011_final.pdf

BOX 8
Examples of Hotlines for Victims of Human Trafficking

The National Human Trafficking Resource Center (NHTRC) is a 24-hour national hotline funded by HHS and operated through a cooperative agreement with Polaris Project. This hotline answers crisis calls (e.g., from trafficking victims in need of immediate assistance), provides referrals to local victim and support services, receives tips related to human trafficking, and responds to inquiries for general information and technical assistance.

FOR MORE INFORMATION:

Polaris Project. 2013. National Human Trafficking Resource Center.
http://www.polarisproject.org/what-we-do/national-human-trafficking-hotline/the-nhtrc/overview

In Chicago, the Salvation Army's STOP-IT Initiative Against Human Trafficking, discussed in Box 7, operates a 24-hour hotline. This hotline helps connect callers with local service providers. There also are hotlines that exist exclusively to assist commercially sexually exploited youth. One example is a hotline operated by Courtney's House, also discussed in Box 7. This hotline, which connects victims with local resources, is answered by survivors of commercial sexual exploitation.

FOR MORE INFORMATION:

STOP-IT Initiative Against Human Trafficking.
http://sa-stopit.org

Courtney's House.
http://www.courtneyshouse.org

MULTISECTOR AND INTERAGENCY EFFORTS

Each of the sectors involved in addressing commercial sexual exploitation and sex trafficking of minors—victim and support services, health care, education, the legal sector, and the commercial sector—has specific roles to play. As noted earlier, however, an adequate response to these crimes requires collaboration and coordination among all of these sectors, as well as at all levels—federal, state, and local. Yet the efforts of individuals, groups, and organizations in different sectors and with different areas of expertise tend to be disconnected. The IOM/NRC report highlights a number of examples of initiatives that have overcome this barrier to a comprehensive response.

Models from Other Domains

Because of the lack of research and evaluation of collaborative initiatives to address commercial sexual exploitation and sex trafficking of minors, the IOM/NRC report describes such initiatives in the related domains of child maltreatment, domestic violence, and sexual assault, all of which involve providers of victim and support services:

- **Child maltreatment**—Children's advocacy centers centralize and coordinate the investigation of child abuse cases and related social services and mental health care, as well as advocacy services [18]. They require the use of multidisciplinary teams that include law enforcement investigators, child protection workers, prosecutors, and mental health and other health care professionals, among others, to coordinate forensic interviews, medical evaluations, therapeutic interventions, and victim advocacy.

  FOR MORE INFORMATION:

  Kristi House. 2012. Commercial Sexual Exploitation.
  http://www.kristihouse.org/commercial-sexual-exploitation

  National Children's Alliance. 2013. History of National Children's Alliance.
  http://www.nationalchildrensalliance.org/index.php?s=35

- **Domestic violence**—In a family justice center, as in a children's advocacy center, a multidisciplinary team of professionals is co-located and works together to provide coordinated care to victims of domestic violence [19]. Services encompass advocacy, interviews with law enforcement personnel, medical assistance, information on shelter, and help with transportation.

  FOR MORE INFORMATION:

  Family Justice Center Alliance. 2013. What Is a Family Justice Center?
  http://familyjusticecenter.com/home.html

- **Sexual assault**—Sexual assault response teams are community-based interventions that provide comprehensive care to victims of sexual assault and coordinate the legal, medical, mental health, and advocacy response [20]. They represent a shift from a case focus to a victim/survivor focus [21, 22]. Their activities include conducting multidisciplinary training, providing direct support and advocacy to victims and survivors, developing protocols and policies for responding to cases, conducting case review to coordinate the response to cases, and educating the public about sexual violence and resources available to survivors [23].

Multisector and Interagency Initiatives Addressing Commercial Sexual Exploitation and Sex Trafficking of Minors

Multisector and interagency efforts to address commercial sexual exploitation and sex trafficking of minors at the federal level include task forces and other partnerships, such as those mandated by the 2013 reauthorization of the TVPA [2, 11, 24, 25].

FOR MORE INFORMATION:

BJA (Bureau of Justice Assistance). 2013. Anti-Human Trafficking Task Force Initiative.
https://www.bja.gov/ProgramDetails.aspx?Program_ID=51

Cook County Human Trafficking Task Force.
http://www.cookcountytaskforce.org

OVC (Office for Victims of Crime). 2013. OVC-Funded Grantee Programs to Help Victims of Trafficking.
http://www.ojp.gov/ovc/grants/traffickingmatrix.html

OVC and BJA. 2011. Anti-Human Trafficking Task Force Strategy and Operations E-guide.
https://www.ovcttac.gov/TaskForceGuide/EGuide/Default.aspx

OVC and BJA. 2013. Enhanced Collaborative Model to Combat Human Trafficking FY 2013 Competitive Grant Announcement.
https://www.bja.gov/Funding/13HumanTraffickingSol.pdf

President's Interagency Task Force to Monitor and Combat Trafficking in Persons. 2013. Federal Strategic Action Plan on Services for Victims of Human Trafficking in the United States 2013-2017.
http://ideascale.com//userimages/accounts/91/912839/Victim-Services-SAP-2013-04-09-Public-Comment-B.pdf

U.S. Attorney's Office for the District of Columbia. 2013. The D.C. Human Trafficking Task Force.
http://www.justice.gov/usao/dc/programs/cp/human_trafficking.html

U.S. Department of State. 2012. Annual Meeting of the President's Interagency Task Force to Monitor and Combat Trafficking in Persons.
http://www.state.gov/j/tip/rls/reports/pitf/

Examples of state and local efforts include the following:

- **Washington State**—Washington state's statewide Model Protocol for Commercially Sexually Exploited Children for responding to cases of commercial sexual exploitation and sex trafficking of minors is focused on fostering collaboration and coordination among agencies, improving identification of these crimes, providing services to victims and survivors, holding exploiters accountable, and working toward ending these crimes in the state [26]. The protocol calls for use of a victim-centered approach by law enforcement, the courts, victim advocacy organizations, youth service agencies, and other youth-serving professionals to ensure that victims of these crimes are treated as such rather than as criminals. The protocol encourages multisector collaboration through state, regional, and local efforts. For example, it calls for the use of multidisciplinary teams to provide immediate consultation on cases of commercial sexual exploitation and sex trafficking of minors as they arise and to participate in meetings to share information and collaborate in the management of each ongoing case.

  FOR MORE INFORMATION:

  Washington State Model Protocol for Commercially Sexually Exploited Children.
  http://www.ccyj.org/Project%20Respect%20protocol.pdf

- **Multnomah County, Oregon**—In 2008, Multnomah County initiated a coordinated multisector response to commercial sexual exploitation and sex trafficking of minors. Specific work groups focus on legislation, assistance for victims and survivors, law enforcement practices (e.g., arrests, investigation, and prosecution of exploiters and traffickers), and physical and mental health care. Steering committee members include law enforcement; the district attorney's office; the Departments of Health, Community Justice, and Human Services; survivors; and nongovernmental service providers. Several strategies are used to ensure collaboration across agencies and among various systems. For example, the county created a special unit within the state child welfare agency for victims and survivors of these crimes [27, 28].

FOR MORE INFORMATION:

Multnomah County Community Response to Commercial Sexual Exploitation of Children.
https://multco.us/csec

- **Suffolk County, Massachusetts**—In Suffolk County, more than 35 public and private agencies participate in the Support to End Exploitation Now (SEEN) Coalition. SEEN's multisector, coordinated approach to identifying and serving high-risk and sexually exploited minors includes three components: (1) cross-system collaboration, (2) a trauma-informed continuum of care (see Section 4), and (3) training for professionals who work with children and adolescents. To facilitate collaboration and communication among coalition members, SEEN established formal relationships and protocols, including a steering committee and advisory group, multidisciplinary teams of professionals, and a case coordinator who serves as the central point of contact for all reported victims of commercial sexual exploitation and sex trafficking [5].

FOR MORE INFORMATION:

Support to End Exploitation Now (SEEN) Coalition.
http://www.suffolkcac.org/programs/seen

- **Alameda County, California**—H.E.A.T. (Human Exploitation and Trafficking) Watch is a multidisciplinary, multisystem program that brings together individuals and agencies from law enforcement, health care, advocacy, victim and support services, the courts, probation agencies, the commercial sector, and the community to (1) ensure the safety of victims and survivors and (2) pursue accountability for exploiters and traffickers. Strategies employed by H.E.A.T. Watch include, among others, stimulating community engagement, coordinating training and information sharing, and coordinating the delivery of victim and support services. The program uses a multisector approach to coordinate the delivery of support services. For example, multidisciplinary case review (modeled on the multidisciplinary team approach) is used to create emergency and long-term safety plans.

Referrals for case review are made by law enforcement, prosecutors, probation officials, and social service organizations that have come into contact with these youth. This approach enables members of the multidisciplinary team to share confidential information with agencies that can assist youth in need of services and support.

FOR MORE INFORMATION:

Alameda County District Attorney's Office. 2012. H.E.A.T. Watch Program Blueprint.
http://www.heat-watch.org/heat_watch

4 **Approaches and
Challenges to
Service Provision**

This section describes three approaches to providing victim and support services for victims and survivors of commercial sexual exploitation and sex trafficking of minors: (1) trauma-informed care, (2) case management, and (3) survivor-led and survivor-informed models. As is the case for the initiatives discussed in Section 3, research and evaluation of these approaches is sparse. Thus, the discussion here draws on research from related domains, such as sexual assault and domestic and partner violence. (Box 9 describes one program that reflects recognition of the value of these approaches and of the interrelatedness of commercial sexual exploitation and sex trafficking, intimate partner violence, and sexual abuse.) This section ends with a review of challenges to the provision of victim and support services that must be overcome if victims and survivors are to receive the services they need.

APPROACHES TO THE PROVISION OF SERVICES

Trauma-Informed Care

Trauma-informed care (also referred to as trauma-specific treatment and trauma-focused services) is based on recognizing and addressing the symptoms that commonly occur in response to multiple forms of trauma [29, 30]. Given the nature of abuse and violence experienced by victims and survivors of commercial sexual exploitation and sex trafficking—including exposure to repeated physical, sexual, and in some cases psychological abuse or witnessing violence—services specifically designed to address trauma can provide much-needed help.

BOX 9
Mount Sinai Sexual Assault and Violence
Intervention (SAVI) Program

The SAVI Program is a hospital-based violence prevention and intervention program that has expanded its scope of work to include services and support for victims and survivors of commercial sexual exploitation and sex trafficking. This expansion is based on SAVI's recognition of the associations among sexual abuse, intimate partner violence, and commercial sexual exploitation and sex trafficking. SAVI offers individual trauma-informed counseling, group and family counseling, and case management to victims and survivors of commercial sexual exploitation and sex trafficking. It also connects victims and survivors with community resources to provide support for education and job training, assistance in the process of applying for public benefits, legal advocacy and services, and health care services. SAVI clinicians coordinate services with partners in the Mount Sinai Medical Center, including the Mount Sinai Adolescent Health Center, and with community-based resources, such as GEMS (discussed in Box 6 in Section 3) [23].

FOR MORE INFORMATION:

Mount Sinai Sexual Assault and Violence Intervention (SAVI) Program.
http://www.mountsinai.org/patient-care/service-areas/community-medicine/areas-of-care/
sexual-assault-and-violence-intervention-program-savi

Experiences with trauma can exceed a person's ability to cope, and often have adverse impacts on health and behavior that can last long into the future. Symptoms may include depression, anxiety, anger, disassociation, fearfulness, hopelessness, poor self-image, distrust of the environment, and difficulty maintaining healthy interpersonal relationships [31]. Without treatment, traumatic experiences can lead to changes in the brain that may create an inherent sense of distrust toward others, including those trying to help; a distrust of authority; and a sense of betrayal and resentment toward society in general [32].

According to the Substance Abuse and Mental Health Services Administration, the design of trauma-informed systems of care is "based on an understanding of the vulnerabilities or triggers of trauma survivors that traditional service delivery approaches may exacerbate, so that these services and programs can be more supportive and avoid re-traumatization." Elements of such a system include ongoing training in trauma for staff and leadership, use of trauma assessment tools and provision of trauma-specific services, an environment that is physically and psychologically safe, and meaningful participation by both staff and those receiving services in the design and operation of the organization [33].

Evidence supports the effectiveness of trauma-specific services for victims and survivors of childhood sexual abuse and complex trauma and for women with criminal justice involvement. Trauma-specific services have also been evaluated and found to be effective for women experiencing co-occurring disorders, including substance abuse and depression. The IOM/NRC report notes that trauma-informed care is standard practice for many providers of services to victims and survivors of commercial sexual exploitation and sex trafficking [34, 35, 36, 37, 38].

FOR MORE INFORMATION:

SAMHSA. 2012. Working Definition of Trauma and Principles and Guidance for a Trauma-Informed Approach.
http://www.samhsa.gov/traumajustice/traumadefinition/index.aspx

> "Given the nature of abuse and violence experienced by victims and survivors of commercial sexual exploitation and sex trafficking—including exposure to repeated physical, sexual, and in some cases psychological abuse or witnessing violence—services specifically designed to address trauma can provide much-needed help."

Case Management

Through case management, an individual in need of assistance receives support from a professional—often a case manager—who develops a service plan and serves as a central point of contact for a range of service providers and systems. This professional can assess an individual's needs and identify and coordinate services on his or her behalf. Case management can be especially beneficial for those who have complex needs (e.g., health care, mental health services, legal services) or must interact with multiple systems (e.g., criminal/juvenile justice, child protective services, foster care). As noted in Section 3, case management is a common component of a multidisciplinary team approach to assisting victims and survivors of domestic abuse, child abuse, and sexual assault. The IOM/NRC report notes that many providers of services for victims and survivors of commercial sexual exploitation and sex trafficking use and/or support the use of case management [39].

FOR MORE INFORMATION:

Clawson and Dutch. 2008. Case management and the victim of human trafficking: A critical service for client success.
http://aspe.hhs.gov/hsp/07/humantrafficking/CaseMgmt/ib.htm

"Case management can be especially beneficial for those who have complex needs (e.g., health care, mental health services, legal services) or must interact with multiple systems (e.g., criminal/juvenile justice, child protective services, foster care)."

Survivor-Led and Survivor-Informed Models

Many providers of services for victims and survivors of commercial sexual exploitation and sex trafficking also use and/or support the use of survivor-led and survivor-informed models. For example, survivor-led services and programs are central to GEMS (discussed in Section 3). Youth leadership by survivors of commercial sexual exploitation and sex trafficking was found to be important to the personal growth and development of GEMS participants. According to one service provider quoted in the IOM/NRC report: "It is also such a testament to the youth to be able to see people, and have tangible conversations, and interact with people who can say, 'Yes I have been there. It is possible to get out. It doesn't always have to be this way.'"

FOR MORE INFORMATION:

GEMS (Girls Educational & Mentoring Services).
http://www.gems-girls.org

Motivating, Inspiring, Supporting and Serving Sexually Exploited Youth (MISSSEY).
http://www.misssey.org

CHALLENGES TO SERVICE PROVISION

Providers of services to victims and survivors of commercial sexual exploitation and sex trafficking generally agree that too few services are available to meet current needs. Moreover, the services that do exist are unevenly distributed geographically, lack adequate resources, and vary in their ability to provide specialized care. Some of the challenges to adequate service provision are summarized in this section. The IOM/NRC report stresses the importance of conducting research to identify ways of overcoming these challenges.

"Providers of services to victims and survivors of commercial sexual exploitation and sex trafficking generally agree that too few services are available to meet current needs."

Lack of Adequate Shelter and Housing

Many law enforcement personnel familiar with sex trafficking cases identify shelter and housing as the most needed service for victims [40]. Yet emergency, short-term, and long-term housing for victims of commercial sexual exploitation and sex trafficking is limited, and in many parts of the country is nonexistent [15, 41, 42, 43, 44, 45, 46, 47, 48, 49]. Appropriate and acceptable shelter options are in particularly short supply for certain groups [50, 51]. For example, transgender youth may not be given the opportunity to designate the sex-specific housing with which they identify, potentially exposing them to violence and/or discrimination.

Few Victim and Support Services for Boys

Few victim and support service providers work with male victims and survivors of commercial sexual exploitation and sex trafficking [42]. As noted in Section 3, there is growing recognition that boys and young men are victims and survivors of these crimes, and greater attention is needed to preventing and identifying these crimes among these youth and providing them with gender-specific services.

Lack of Awareness Among Service Providers

As noted in Section 3, victim and support service providers working with vulnerable youth may not recognize those in their care who have experienced or are at risk of commercial sexual exploitation and sex trafficking. As a result, they may fail to connect these youth to appropriate and timely services. Section 3 describes efforts to train service providers in and raise public awareness of these crimes. Broadening the reach of these existing efforts is one strategy for increasing understanding and recognition of the problem.

Lack of Information Sharing and Communication

Victims and survivors of commercial sexual exploitation and sex trafficking may require a range of victim and support services (e.g., mental health and substance abuse services, housing/shelter). Unfortunately, information sharing and communication may be lacking among the various providers of these services. Multisector collaboration (discussed in Section 3) and case management (discussed on page 35) are potential strategies for closing this gap.

Impact on Service Providers of Working with Victims and Survivors

Professionals may experience negative effects from working with vulnerable and traumatized individuals [52, 53, 54]. These effects include impacts on physical and psychological health [55], burnout, and secondary traumatic stress (e.g., sleep disturbance).

Lack of Consensus on Services and Service Delivery

While there is some agreement on specific services needed, consensus currently is lacking on the range of services that should be available to assist and support victims and survivors of commercial sexual exploitation and sex trafficking effectively over time. Consensus is also lacking on the most effective or efficient model of service delivery for victims and survivors of these crimes.

5 Recommended Strategies

"The human cost of the status quo is
simply unacceptable."

The IOM/NRC report concludes with a series of recommendations for making progress toward preventing and responding to commercial sexual exploitation and sex trafficking of minors in the United States. The strategies for progress articulated in the report's recommendations are summarized in this section.

INCREASE AWARENESS AND UNDERSTANDING

As discussed in prior sections, a lack of training among professionals who interact with children and adolescents—especially those who are vulnerable—is a barrier to timely and appropriate action to assist victims and survivors of commercial sexual exploitation and sex trafficking and prevent these crimes among youth at risk. These professionals are often dismayed to learn that they have missed opportunities to help these youth and want to know more about how to identify and assist them.

Training

Training for professionals and others who interact with young people needs to target and reach a range of audiences in a variety of settings (e.g., urban

**RECOMMENDATION TO INCREASE
AWARENESS AND UNDERSTANDING**

Develop, implement, and evaluate:

- training for professionals and others who routinely interact with children and adolescents,
- public awareness campaigns, and
- specific strategies for children and adolescents.

and rural; tribal lands, territories, and states). Relevant sectors (e.g., health care, law enforcement, victim and support services) should participate in the development, implementation, and evaluation of training activities that use evidence-based methods. Further, each sector should be consulted to determine the best methods for that sector, given that needs may vary, for example, between law enforcement personnel and health care providers.

Public Awareness Campaigns

A lack of public awareness is a significant barrier to preventing, identifying, and responding to commercial sexual exploitation and sex trafficking of minors in the United States. To address this gap, existing public awareness initiatives could be expanded to encompass these crimes.

Strategies for Awareness Among Children and Adolescents

Child and adolescent victims and survivors of commercial sexual exploitation and sex trafficking may not view themselves as victims, and youth who are at risk for this kind of exploitation may not recognize their individual risk. Therefore, special efforts are needed to increase the awareness of children and adolescents to help them avoid becoming victims and to help victims and survivors obtain the assistance they need.

STRENGTHEN THE LAW'S RESPONSE

"Individuals who sexually exploit children and adolescents have largely escaped accountability."

A small but growing number of states have enacted laws—sometimes referred to as "safe harbor" laws—designed to redirect young victims of commercial sexual exploitation and sex trafficking from the criminal or juvenile justice system to child welfare or other agencies to receive supportive services. While recognizing that additional time and research are needed to assess the effectiveness of specific state laws, the IOM/NRC report recommends that the core principle underlying these safe harbor laws—that children and adolescents who are survivors of sexual exploitation and sex trafficking must be treated as victims, not criminals—should be advanced without delay.

In addition, despite laws in every state that enable the prosecution of individuals who purchase sex with a minor, function as exploiters/traffickers, or otherwise sexually exploit children and adolescents, and despite the hard work of prosecutors and law enforcement in many jurisdictions, individuals who sexually exploit children and adolescents have largely escaped accountability.

RECOMMENDATIONS TO STRENGTHEN THE LAW'S RESPONSE

Develop laws and policies that **redirect** young victims and survivors of commercial sexual exploitation and sex trafficking from arrest and prosecution to systems, agencies, and services that are equipped to meet their needs. *Such laws should apply to all children and adolescents under age 18.*

Review, strengthen, and implement laws that hold exploiters, traffickers, and solicitors **accountable** for their role in commercial sexual exploitation and sex trafficking of minors. *These laws should include a particular emphasis on deterring demand.*

STRENGTHEN RESEARCH ON PREVENTION AND INTERVENTION

As noted previously, the evidence base on strategies and approaches for preventing and responding to commercial sexual exploitation and sex trafficking of minors in the United States is extremely limited.

RECOMMENDATION TO STRENGTHEN RESEARCH ON PREVENTION AND INTERVENTION

Implement a national research agenda focused on:

- advancing knowledge and understanding;
- developing effective interventions; and
- evaluating the effectiveness of prevention and intervention laws, policies, and programs.

SUPPORT COLLABORATION

As discussed in Section 3, collaborative, coordinated approaches that bring together resources from multiple sectors will be most effective in identifying victims and survivors and in meeting their challenging needs.

RECOMMENDATION TO SUPPORT COLLABORATION AND COORDINATION

Develop **guidelines** on and provide **technical assistance** to support multisector collaboration and coordination.

SUPPORT INFORMATION SHARING

"The difficulty of locating services and programs available to victims is a very real obstacle for children and adolescents seeking to access services and for professionals and caregivers trying to help them."

One of the most significant barriers to preventing, identifying, and responding to commercial sexual exploitation and sex trafficking of minors is a lack of reliable, timely information. A number of organizations maintain lists of services available to child and adolescent victims of commercial sexual exploitation and sex trafficking. However, there is no exhaustive list of national-, state-, local-, and tribal-level resources for victim and support services. The difficulty of locating services and programs available to victims is a very real obstacle for children and adolescents seeking to access services and for professionals and caregivers trying to help them.

RECOMMENDATION TO SUPPORT INFORMATION SHARING

Create and maintain a digital information-sharing platform to deliver **reliable, real-time information** on how to prevent, identify, and respond to commercial sexual exploitation and sex trafficking of minors in the United States.

FINAL THOUGHTS

Efforts to prevent, identify, and respond to commercial sexual exploitation and sex trafficking of minors in the United States are in the same developmental stage that efforts to deal with physical and sexual abuse of children were in during the 1970s, when a handful of multidisciplinary approaches for addressing those problems were emerging around the country. Approaches to domestic and interpersonal violence were at a similar stage in the early 1980s. The nation today has a real opportunity to build on lessons from those earlier efforts, as well as current noteworthy practices, to address the problem of commercial sexual exploitation and sex trafficking of minors, and the victim and support services sector has a crucial role to play in achieving this goal. The children and adolescents who are at risk and are victims and survivors of these crimes cannot wait. The human cost of the status quo is simply unacceptable.

References

1. Adams, S. 2012. Workshop presentation to the Committee on the Commercial Sexual Exploitation and Sex Trafficking of Minors in the United States, on the Larkin Street Youth Services, May 9, San Francisco, CA.
2. Walts, K. K., S. French, H. Moore, and S. Ashai. 2011. *Building child welfare response to child trafficking.* Chicago, IL: Loyola University Chicago, Center for the Human Rights of Children.
3. Child Welfare Information Gateway. 2013. *Fact sheet: How the child welfare system works.* https://www.childwelfare.gov/pubs/factsheets/cpswork.pdf (accessed April 25, 2013).
4. Dorsey, S., S. E. U. Kerns, E. W. Trupin, K. L. Conover, and L. Berliner. 2012. Child welfare caseworkers as service brokers for youth in foster care: Findings from Project Focus. *Child Maltreatment* 17(1):22-31.
5. Piening, S., and T. Cross. 2012. *From "the life" to my life: Sexually exploited children reclaiming their futures. Suffolk County Massachusetts' response to commercial sexual exploitation of children (CSEC).* Boston, MA: Children's Advocacy Center of Suffolk County.
6. Wilson, J. M., and E. Dalton. 2008. Human trafficking in the heartland. *Journal of Contemporary Criminal Justice* 24(3):296-313.
7. HHS (U.S. Department of Health and Human Services). 2012. *Services available to victims of human trafficking: A resource guide for social service providers.* Washington, DC: HHS.
8. My Life, My Choice. 2012. *Preventing the exploitation of girls: A groundbreaking curriculum.* Boston, MA: Justice Research Institute.
9. Goldblatt Grace, L. 2012. Site visit presentation to the Committee on the Commercial Sexual Exploitation and Sex Trafficking of Minors in the United States, on My Life, My Choice, March 23, Boston, MA.

10. Frundt, T. 2012. Presentation to the Committee on the Commercial Sexual Exploitation and Sex Trafficking of Minors in the United States, on Courtney's House, February 29, Washington, DC.

11. Knowles-Wirsing, E. 2012. Site visit presentation to the Committee on the Commercial Sexual Exploitation and Sex Trafficking of Minors in the United States, on The Salvation Army's STOP-IT Initiative, July 11, Chicago, IL.

12. Larkin Street Youth Services. 2011. *Larkin Street Youth Services 2011 annual report.* San Francisco, CA: Larkin Street Youth Services.

13. Shared Hope International. 2006. *Demand: A comparative examination of sex tourism and trafficking in Jamaica, Japan, the Netherlands, and the United States.* Vancouver, WA: Shared Hope International.

14. Smith, L., S. H. Vardaman, and M. A. Snow. 2009. *The national report on domestic minor sex trafficking: America's prostituted children.* Vancouver, WA: Shared Hope International.

15. Shared Hope International. 2012. *Protected innocence challenge: State report cards on the legal framework of protection for the nation's children.* Vancouver, WA: Shared Hope International.

16. Smolenski, C. 2012. Workshop presentation to the Committee on the Commercial Sexual Exploitaiton and Sex Trafficking of Minors in the United States, on the ECPAT-USA Code of Conduct, May 9, San Francisco, CA.

17. Dunn Burque, A. 2009. *Empowering young men to end sexual exploitation: Report, curriculum, and recommended resources.* Chicago, IL: Chicago Alliance Against Sexual Exploitation.

18. Cross, T. P., L. M. Jones, W. A. Walsh, M. Simone, D. J. Kolko, J. Szczepanski, T. Lippert, K. Davison, A. Cryns, P. Sosnowski, A. Shadoin, and S. Magnuson. 2008. *Evaluating children's advocacy centers' response to child sexual abuse.* Washington, DC: U.S. Department of Justice, Office of Juvenile Justice and Delinquency Prevention.

19. Gwinn, C., G. Strack, S. Adams, R. Lovelace, and D. Norman. 2007. The Family Justice Center Collaborative Model. *Saint Louis University Public Law Review 79.*

20. Greeson, M. R., and R. Campbell. 2013. Sexual Assault Response Teams (SARTs): An empirical review of their effectiveness and challenges to successful implementation. *Trauma, Violence, and Abuse* 14(2):83-95.

21. Latimer, D. 2012. Site visit presentation to the Committee on the Commercial Sexual Exploitation and Sex Trafficking of Minors in the United States, Mount Sinai Sexual Assault and Violence Intervention (SAVI) Program, September 12, New York.

22. National Sexual Violence Resource Center. 2006. *Report on the national needs assessment of sexual assault response teams.* Enola, PA: National Sexual Violence Resource Center.

23. Zajac, J. 2009. *National Sexual Assault Response Team survey report 2009.* Enola, PA: National Sexual Violence Resource Center.

24. Greene, J. 2012. Site visit presentation to the Committee on the Commercial Sexual Exploitation and Sex Trafficking of Minors in the United States, on Cook County State's Attorney's Office, Human Trafficking Task Force, July 11, Chicago, IL.

25. Nasser, M. 2012. Site visit presentation to the Committee on the Commercial Sexual Exploitation and Sex Trafficking of Minors in the United States, on the U.S. Attorney's Office, Northern District of Illinois, July 11, Chicago, IL.

26. Bridge, B. J., N. Oakley, L. Briner, and B. Graef. 2012. *Washington state model protocol for commercially sexually exploited children.* Seattle, WA: Center for Children and Youth Justice.

27. Baker, J., and E. Nelson. 2012. Workshop presentation to the Committee on the Commercial Sexual Exploitation and Sex Trafficking of Minors in the United States, on multi-disciplinary responses, May 9, San Francisco, CA.

28. Multnomah County. 2012. *Multnomah County: Community response to commercial sexual exploitation of children (CSEC).* Multnomah County, OR: Department of Community Justice.

29. Johnson, N. L., and D. M. Johnson. 2013. Factors influencing the relationship between sexual trauma and risky sexual behavior in college students. *Journal of Interpersonal Violence* 28(11):2315-2331.

30. Zerk, D., P. Mertin, and M. Proeve. 2009. Domestic violence and maternal reports of young children's functioning. *Journal of Family Violence* 24(7):423-432.

31. Fortier, M. A., D. DiLillo, T. L. Messman-Moore, J. Peugh, K. A. DeNardi, and K. J. Gaffey. 2009. Severity of child sexual abuse and revictimization: The mediating role of coping and trauma symptoms. *Psychology of Women Quarterly* 33(3):308-320.

32. DOJ (U.S. Department of Justice). 2012. *Report of the Attorney General's National Task Force on Children Exposed to Violence.* Washington, DC: DOJ.

33. Guarino, K., P. Soares, K. Konnath, R. Clervil, and E. Bassuk. 2009. *Trauma-informed organizational toolkit.* Rockville, MD: Center for Mental Health Services, Substance Abuse and Mental Health Services Administration, and the Daniels Fund, the National Child Traumatic Stress Network, and the W.K. Kellogg Foundation.

34. Cohen, J. A., A. P. Mannarino, M. Kliethermes, and L. A. Murray. 2012. Trauma-focused CBT for youth with complex trauma. *Child Abuse and Neglect* 36(6):528-541.

35. Conradi, L., and C. Wilson. 2010. Managing traumatized children: A trauma systems perspective. *Current Opinion in Pediatrics* 22(5):621-625.

36. Covington, S. S., C. Burke, S. Keaton, and C. Norcott. 2008. Evaluation of a trauma-informed and gender-responsive intervention for women in drug treatment. *Journal of Psychoactive Drugs* (Suppl. 5):387-398.

37. Olafson, E. 2011. Child sexual abuse: Demography, impact, and interventions. *Journal of Child and Adolescent Trauma* 4(1):8-21.

38. Schneider, S. J., S. F. Grilli, and J. R. Schneider. 2013. Evidence-based treatments for traumatized children and adolescents. *Current Psychiatry Reports* 15(1):332-341.

39. Clawson, H. J., and N. Dutch. 2008. *Case management and the victim of human trafficking: A critical service for client success.* Washington, DC: HHS, Office of the Assistant Secretary for Planning and Evaluation.

40. Clawson, H. J., N. Dutch, and M. Cummings. 2006. *Law enforcement response to human trafficking and the implications for victims: Current practices and lessons learned.* Fairfax, VA: Caliber.

41. Aron, L. Y., J. M. Zweig, and L. C. Newmark. 2006. *Comprehensive services for survivors of human trafficking: Findings from clients in three communities.* Washington, DC: Urban Institute Justice Policy Center.

42. Clawson, H. J., N. M. Dutch, A. Solomon, and L. Goldblatt Grace. 2009. *Human trafficking into and within the United States: A review of the literature.* Washington, DC: HHS, Office of the Assistant Secretary for Planning and Evaluation.

43. Clawson, H. J., N. M. Dutch, A. Solomon, and L. Goldblatt Grace. 2009. *Study of HHS programs serving human trafficking victims.* Washington, DC: HHS, Office of the Assistant Secretary for Planning and Evaluation.

44. Clawson, H. J., and L. Goldblatt Grace. 2007. *Finding a path to recovery: Residential facilities for minor victims of domestic sex trafficking.* Washington, DC: HHS, Office of the Assistant Secretary for Planning and Evaluation.

45. Ferguson, K. M., H. Soydan, S. Y. Lee, A. Yamanaka, A. S. Freer, and B. Xie. 2009. Evaluation of the CSEC Community Intervention Project (CCIP) in five U.S. cities. *Evaluation Review* 33(6):568-597.

46. Finklea, K. M., A. L. Fernandes-Alcantara, and A. Siskin. 2011. *Sex trafficking of children in the United States: Overview and issues for Congress.* Washington, DC: Congressional Research Service.

47. Giardino, A. P., and R. D. Sanborn. 2011. Human trafficking: Awareness, data and policy. *Journal of Applied Research on Children: Informing Policy for Children at Risk* 2(1).

48. Gragg, F., I. Petta, H. Bernstein, K. Eisen, and L. Quinn. 2007. *New York prevalence study of commercially sexually exploited children.* Rensselaer, NY: New York State Office of Children and Family Services.

49. Polaris Project. 2012. *Shelter beds for human trafficking survivors in the United States.* https://na4.salesforce.com/sfc/p/300000006E4S9liF7eeqnplT97HRFH4FvCSI5v4= (accessed April 30, 2013).

50. Holzman, J. 2012. Site visit presentation to the Committee on the Commercial Sexual Exploitation and Sex Trafficking of Minors in the United States, on the Girls Educational and Mentoring Services (GEMS) services and programs, September 12, New York.

51. Westmacott, J. 2012. Site visit presentation to the Committee on the Commercial Sexual Exploitation and Sex Trafficking of Minors in the United States, Safe Horizon, September 12, New York.

52. Cornille, T. A., and T. W. Meyers. 1999. Secondary traumatic stress among child protective service workers: Prevalence, severity, and predictive factors. *Traumatology* 5(1):15-31.

53. Pearlman, L. A., and P. S. Mac Ian. 1995. Vicarious traumatization: An empirical study of the effects of trauma work on trauma therapists. *Professional Psychology: Research and Practice* 26(6):558-565.

54. Salston, M., and C. R. Figley. 2003. Secondary traumatic stress effects of working with survivors of criminal victimization. *Journal of Traumatic Stress* 16(2):167.

55. Kliner, M., and L. Stroud. 2012. Psychological and health impact of working with victims of sex trafficking. *Journal of Occupational Health* 54(1):9.